HIKING

BY SARA GREEN

BELLWETHER MEDIA • MINNEAPOLIS, MN

Jump into the cockpit and take flight with Pilot books. Your journey will take you on high-energy adventures as you learn about all that is wild, weird, fascinating, and fun!

This edition first published in 2013 by Bellwether Media, Inc.

No part of this publication may be reproduced in whole or in part without written permission of the publisher. For information regarding permission, write to Bellwether Media, Inc., Attention: Permissions Department, 5357 Penn Avenue South, Minneapolis, MN 55419.

Library of Congress Cataloging-in-Publication Data

Green, Sara, 1964-
Hiking / by Sara Green.
     p. cm. – (Pilot books: outdoor adventures)
Includes bibliographical references and index.
 Summary: "Engaging images accompany information about hiking. The combination of high-interest subject matter and narrative text is intended for students in grades 3 through 7"–Provided by publisher.
 ISBN 978-1-60014-800-2 (hardcover : alk. paper)
 1. Hiking–Juvenile literature. I. Title.
 GV199.52.G74 2012
 796.52–dc23

                                     2012013440

Printed in the United States of America, North Mankato, MN.

TABLE OF CONTENTS

A Natural Reward 4

Gearing Up 10

Hitting the Trail 16

The Appalachian Trail 20

Glossary 22

To Learn More 23

Index 24

A NATURAL REWARD

Several hikers make their way down a trail in the woods. They are hiking to a famous lookout. Along the way they see deer, foxes, rabbits, and other wildlife. One hiker notices a bird in the distance and looks through her binoculars. Another hiker sees a bright flower and uses a book to identify it.

After a few hours, they emerge from the forest. They find themselves in a grassy meadow near a cliff. Far below is a valley with a river winding through it. The hikers sit on rocks that face the valley. One hiker passes around snacks as others pull out their cameras. They will never forget this spot.

Hiking is one of the best ways to explore the natural world. It's a great activity for learning about the geography of an area and the plants and animals that live there. Some people hike to spend time outdoors and breathe fresh air. Others hike to keep their minds and bodies strong. Hiking is a good way to strengthen muscles and boost endurance.

Bright Angel Trail

Desert Challenge

One of the most dangerous hikes in the United States is the Bright Angel Trail in Arizona's Grand Canyon. The 9.5-mile (15.3-kilometer) trail descends 4,380 feet (1,335 meters)!

Hikes range in difficulty and length. Short hikes that last several hours are called day hikes. Long-distance hikes last several days to several weeks. This kind of hiking is also called backpacking. Backpackers carry large packs filled with gear for camping along the way.

Hikers do not usually have to travel far to find a trailhead. Many cities offer a variety of hiking trails that wind through parks and around lakes. These trails provide an escape from the noise of the city. People with little spare time can enjoy taking a break in nature.

Those who seek a bigger adventure hike on trails in state and national parks. Easy trails are short and often paved. Difficult trails are usually longer and may include steep changes in elevation. They may have uneven or slippery terrain. Hikers often navigate large roots, stream crossings, or scree. Many hikers use trekking poles to improve their balance on difficult trails. Trekking poles also help hikers increase their speed.

GEARING UP

Hikers must be prepared for all possible conditions. Sturdy hiking boots keep hikers safe and comfortable for hours on the trail. Layered clothing helps them adjust to changes in weather. Hikers should wear hats and sunscreen during long days in the sun. It is also a good idea to carry a **water-repellent** jacket in case of rain. A fleece jacket comes in handy if the temperature drops.

Day hikers usually carry small backpacks with adjustable straps. These are called daypacks. They are made of a lightweight, water-resistant material and are large enough to hold basic supplies. Daypacks often have pockets for easy access to items such as water bottles, maps, and snacks. Hikers should always check the fit and weight of their daypacks before heading out on the trail.

Hiker's Best Friend

Some dog breeds make great hiking companions. They can even carry a few items in their own small backpacks!

All hikers must drink plenty of water to prevent **dehydration**. Day hikers should bring enough to last the entire hike. They must also eat enough food to keep their energy high. Trail mix, bagels, and dried fruit are great energy-boosting snacks to pack. Many day hikers choose to eat sandwiches at a scenic spot along the trail. They rest their feet while enjoying lunch and the view.

Day Hike Checklist

- Water
- Snacks
- Layered clothing
- Basic first aid supplies
- Trail maps and compass
- Sunscreen
- Bug repellent

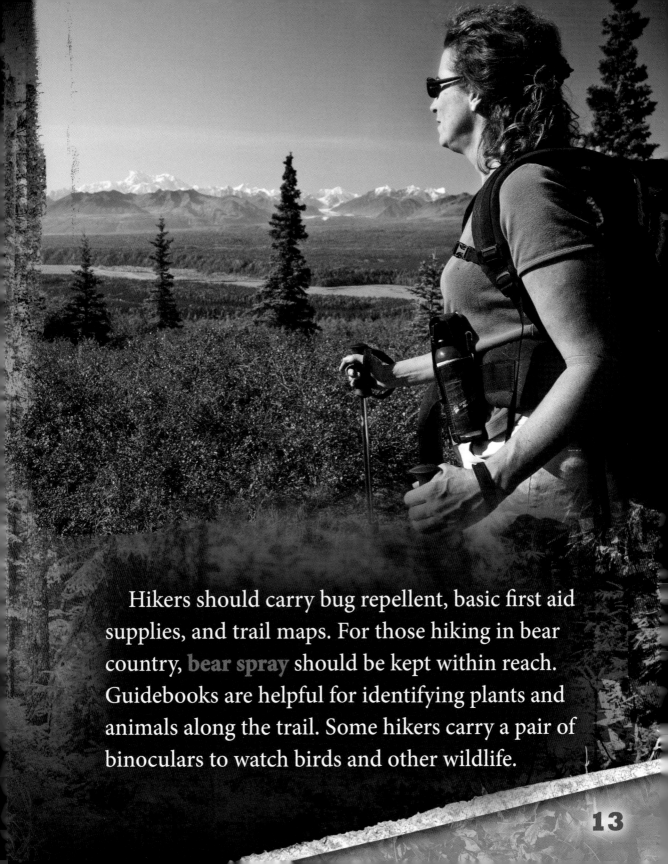

Hikers should carry bug repellent, basic first aid supplies, and trail maps. For those hiking in bear country, **bear spray** should be kept within reach. Guidebooks are helpful for identifying plants and animals along the trail. Some hikers carry a pair of binoculars to watch birds and other wildlife.

Hikers who will be out for two or more days must plan well. Backpacking requires more gear than day hiking. In addition to basic supplies, a backpacker must carry a tent, sleeping bag, and sleeping pad.

Hiking Shape

Carrying a heavy backpack over uneven terrain can be tiring. Walking up and down steep hills can help people get into hiking shape.

Many backpackers carry a small stove and
fuel to cook meals at a campsite. Most prefer
packaged foods that are easy to prepare outdoors.
Backpackers often cannot carry all of the water
they will need. Many bring a water purifier.
This makes water from lakes, streams, and rivers
safe to drink. Backpackers who hike into the
backcountry need to know how to use a map
and compass to avoid getting lost.

HITTING THE TRAIL

Respectful hikers follow a few rules to protect the environment and keep people safe. They stay on clearly marked trails when possible to avoid damaging natural areas. They do not collect rocks, pick flowers, or disturb wildlife. Garbage is never left behind.

Hikers should always tell a friend, family member, or park ranger when and where they are going to hike. They should pick trails that they are confident they can manage. Group hiking is safer than hiking alone. Friends can keep track of one another so nobody gets lost. If one person gets injured, a fellow hiker can apply first aid.

Leave No Trace

Responsible hikers follow the saying, "Take only pictures, leave only footprints." This preserves trails for other hikers.

Sky Hikes

Heli-hiking offers a whole different adventure. Helicopters take people to remote places and guides lead them on hikes with incredible scenery!

Hiking is an activity that can be enjoyed year-round. Beautiful wildflowers color trails in the spring. Summer hikers enjoy birds and other wildlife on shady forest paths. Autumn hikes promise cool, crisp air and vibrant leaves. The quiet of winter is a great time for hikers to identify animal tracks in the snow. No matter where people live, they can find great places to hike. All it takes is some basic gear and preparation before hitting the trail!

THE APPALACHIAN TRAIL

The Appalachian Trail, or A.T., is a famous trail in the eastern United States. It is 2,181 miles (3,510 kilometers) long and passes through fourteen states from Georgia to Maine. The terrain includes mountains, forests, meadows, and swamps.

People come from all over the world to hike this spectacular trail. Some people hike the trail's entire length. This is called thru-hiking. It takes about four to six months to complete a thru-hike on the A.T. These hikers often stay overnight in shelters built alongside the trail. The challenge of completing an A.T. thru-hike is a life goal for many hikers.

trailhead (Maine)

trailhead (Georgia)

N
W E
S

A.T. Hall of Fame

- In 2008, the 10,000th person completed the Appalachian Trail.

- A blind hiker named Bill Irwin completed a thru-hike with his dog, Orient, in 1990.

- In 2004, Lee Barry became the oldest A.T. thru-hiker at 81 years old. The youngest thru-hikers were 6 years old.

GLOSSARY

backcountry—wilderness; backcountry has little to no human development.

bear spray—a spray made from hot peppers; bear spray is used to stop bears from attacking.

dehydration—excessive loss of water from the body

elevation—the height of the land; land elevation is measured against sea level.

endurance—the ability to do something for a long time

geography—the study of the physical features of the earth

lookout—a place where people can look out over a landscape

park ranger—a person who protects and preserves parks; park rangers also enforce park rules.

scree—small, loose stones that cover a slope or mountain

sleeping pad—a cushioned pad that provides comfort and protects a camper from the cold ground

terrain—a stretch of land

trailhead—the starting point of a trail

trekking poles—lightweight poles that keep people stable as they hike

water purifier—a filter or tablet that removes unhealthy materials from water to make it safe to drink

water-repellent—made of material that does not soak up water

TO LEARN MORE

At the Library

Coppin, Sara. *Hiking: Have Fun, Be Smart.* New York, N.Y.: Rosen Pub. Group, 2000.

Klein, Adam G. *Hiking.* Edina, Minn.: ABDO Pub. Co., 2008.

National Geographic Kids. *National Geographic Kids National Parks Guide U.S.A.: The Most Amazing Sights, Scenes, and Cool Activities from Coast to Coast!* Washington, D.C.: National Geographic Society, 2012.

On the Web

Learning more about hiking is as easy as 1, 2, 3.

1. Go to www.factsurfer.com.

2. Enter "hiking" into the search box.

3. Click the "Surf" button and you will see a list of related Web sites.

With factsurfer.com, finding more information is just a click away.

INDEX

American Discovery Trail, 8
Appalachian Trail, 20, 21
backpacking, 7, 14, 15
bear spray, 13
binoculars, 4, 13
Bright Angel Trail, 7
bug repellent, 12, 13
camping, 7, 15
clothing, 10, 12
compass, 12, 15
day hiking, 7, 10, 12, 14
daypacks, 10
dehydration, 12
dogs, 11, 21
endurance, 6
first aid, 12, 13, 17
food, 10, 12, 15
geography, 6
heli-hiking, 18
maps, 10, 12, 13, 15

rules, 17
safety, 10, 12, 13, 15, 17
thru-hiking, 20, 21
trailhead, 8, 20
trekking poles, 9
water purifier, 15
wildlife, 4, 6, 13, 17, 19